The Best 30 Days of Faith: College Edition

Faithful Byrd

TRILOGY CHRISTIAN PUBLISHERS

Tustin, CA

TRILOGY

Trilogy Christian Publishers
A Wholly Owned Subsidary of Trinity Broadcasting Network
2442 Michelle Drive
Tustin, CA 92780

The Best 30 Days of Faith: College Edition

For information, address Trilogy Christian Publishing

Rights Department, 2442 Michelle Drive, Tustin, CA 92780.

Trilogy Christian Publishing/ TBN and colophon are trademarks of Trinity Broadcasting Network.

For information about special discounts for bulk purchases, please contact Trilogy Christian Publishing.

Trilogy Disclaimer: The views and content expressed in this book are those of the author and may not necessarily reflect the views and doctrine of Trilogy Christian Publishing or the Trinity Broadcasting Network.

10 9 8 7 6 5 4 3 2 1

Library of Congress Cataloging-in-Publication Data is available.

ISBN: 979-8-89041-943-9

ISBN: 979-8-89041-944-6 (ebook)

Dedication

Archie & Harriett Byrd (Daddy & Mommy)

To Archie & Harriett Byrd, my God-fearing, top tier parents, who introduced me not just to the concept of Jesus but to a living, breathing relationship with Him – the very source of inspiration behind this devotional. Your unwavering encouragement, constant belief in my dreams, and tireless support have been the guiding light on this remarkable journey. Through your guidance, you instilled in me the profound understanding of not just chasing dreams, but dedicating my gifts and talents to Jesus, the ultimate purpose. With boundless love and heartfelt gratitude, I dedicate this book to both of you. Your profound influence continues to shape every word, and your unwavering support remains the cornerstone of my life's foundation. Thank you for nurturing my faith and loving me unconditionally.

Maranatha and True

To my loving, courageous. beautiful, confident God-fearing sisters. My tribe. Thank you for loving me unconditionally and being the sisters and support team I need in this life. I'm so blessed to have you both in my life. Love always.
- Big Sis

Grandma

To my dear Grandma, your encouragement, delightful phone calls filled with songs, and insightful Bible talks have been my greatest inspiration. Your support has been a guiding force that fueled the completion of this devotional. With heartfelt love and gratitude, thank you for believing in me and being my source of encouragement throughout this journey.

Lighthouse Community SDA Church

My beloved church family at Lighthouse, your unwavering support, love, and sense of community have been much appreciated. I am eternally grateful for your presence in my life. Thank you for being the church family I need. With heartfelt appreciation and love, y'all have truly made a difference.

Florida Seventh-Day Adventist Conference

Dedicated to the Florida Seventh-Day Adventist Conference, whose support and sponsorship made the creation of this book possible. Your commitment to the community and faith has inspired its pages, shaping a work intended to uplift and enlighten.

Contents

Preface

Dear college ladies,

Within the bustling rhythm of collegiate life, amidst the lectures, assignments, and social engagements, we often find our faith journey caught in the whirlwind. As young women navigating the maze of academia and personal growth, the longing for a deeper connection with Jesus can be both palpable and elusive.

I was inspired to create this 30-day devotional by my transformative trip to Argentina, where I had the incredible opportunity to delve deeper into understanding God's character and His unending love. It was a journey that sparked a fire within me to share the profound revelations and experiences I encountered throughout college.

This devotional is a compass, designed to accompany you on this transformative quest. It's a guide for those seeking to not only rediscover Jesus but to forge a more profound and intimate relationship with Him. Each day is a stepping stone, a gentle invitation to reconnect with Christ or deepen your existing bond with Him.

The themes woven through these pages aim to resonate with the unique challenges and triumphs experienced in the college sphere. From the uncertainties of the future to the joys and pressures of relationships, from the quest for purpose to the navigation of academic pursuits – every reflection, prayer, and scripture included seeks to speak directly to your heart.

Above all, may this devotional serve as a daily reminder of Jesus' unwavering presence in your life. He stands ready to walk alongside you through every high and low, offering solace, wisdom, and unending love.

May these devotionals be a quiet retreat amid the college rush, a sanctuary where you can reconnect, reflect, and rejoice in the presence of our beloved Savior, Jesus Christ.

In His boundless love,
Faithful Byrd

Faith as A Mustard Seed

He replied, "Because you have so little faith. Truly I tell you, if you have faith as small as a mustard seed, you can say to this mountain, 'Move from here to there,' and it will move. Nothing will be impossible for you."

Matthew 17:20

Sometimes life has a way of making us feel like there is no hope, nowhere to go, and no one to trust. As a college student, I've felt this way more than once, especially when it comes to financial aid. I remember being in the financial aid office and in need of $3000 to clear. Now, unless you come from wealthy homes or have a rich uncle somewhere, most college students don't have $3,000 just sitting in the bank. I sure didn't!

While the lady was telling me all the things I couldn't do, listing impossibilities as she went, I quietly said to myself, "I can't--but God can, and with Him all things are possible." When I left the financial aid office, I did not become overwhelmed, and I did not hang my head. Instead, I simply prayed to God with faith that He was going to see me through. Literally two hours later, the woman from the aid office called to let me know that she was able to find some more scholarships—enough money for me to be cleared and begin my semester.

The demands of life can be overwhelming, but all God needs from you is faith—and not even a lot of faith: faith as small as a mustard seed. He wants you to have faith in Him and know that even though this mountain might look too steep and high to climb, with God you can fly. So, as you go through your day, remember that as long as you put your faith in God, you give him permission to act exceedingly and abundantly in your life.

Dear Jesus, help me to continue to put my trust in you. I know that life can be very demanding and sometimes it seems like there is no way out, but thank You for the love You have for me. Forgive me for the times I doubted You and put my faith in man. I love You, Lord, and I can't wait to see you soon. In Jesus's name, amen.

Raw Convo with God

How can you integrate faith into your everyday college experiences, relationships, and decision-making processes?

Hot or Cold

"Never let the fire in your heart go out. Keep it alive. Serve the Lord." (Romans 12:11)

One of my favorite gospel songs is "No Gray" by Jonathan McReynolds. The song talks about how he struggles with the cares of the world and wants to participate in worldly things while also giving God his all and living to serve Him. This message really resonates with me as

both a woman and a young Christian trying to make my way in the world. Many of us young

people, myself included, are on the fence when it comes to God. We go out, "turn up," and

then when it is time for church, we are in the pews singing his praises. We are two-faced; one minute we are with the world, and the next we are with God.

I mean, think about it: would you want to be in a relationship with someone who only calls sometimes or only wants to see you occasionally? Of course not! That relationship would not survive a month! It is the exact same way with God. In our Christian walk, we must make a decision to either be hot or cold for Jesus. We cannot serve two masters.

God wants you, and He is willing to meet you where you are, but you must be willing to give up the cares and desires of this world. That might include those friends, that not realize that my actions were causing me to lack peace, joy, and God's blessings. Now I did not want to break up with him; after all, I did love him. However, I knew that what I was doing in the relationship was not brining glory and honor to God. As hard as it was, I broke up with him, and it was hard to make that decision, but I knew I wanted to be on fire for God.

Once I decided to be on fire for God, I had peace, joy and liberation from lustful bondage. If it wasn't for God who comforted me every step of the way, I would not be here writing this book to you. We all have something that makes us straddle the fence, and God knows it. There will be hard times where you want to give up or give into the world, but you must remember His promise to never leave or forsake you. He will always be there to comfort you in your time of need. He will see you through it. The question is: are you willing to give God your all?

Dear Jesus, thank You for being there for me even when I do not deserve it. I am sorry for being on the fence about You and not giving You my all. I do not want to be lukewarm anymore. Instead, I want to be hot for You, Jesus. Continue to come into my heart, forgive me for my sins, and make me more like You. In Jesus name, amen.

I AM

*"I am the Alpha and the Omega,' says the Lord
God, 'who is, and who was, and who is to come, the
Almighty.'"* (Revelation 1:8)

I often try to handle life on my own. It's as if I feel
God is only needed for the big problems such as school
tuition, buying a car, illness, paying bills, etc. I feel as
though I can handle the little problems that come my
way, problems such as a terrible break up, passing a
test, or even getting rid of a headache.

Sometimes, I do not give God a chance to be everything He can be to me: my best friend, my therapist,
my doctor, even a shoulder to cry on. At times I view
God as this mighty being that cannot relate to the little
problems I have in my life, but that is not true. God is
my shoulder to cry on after a terrible break up. He is the
best friend I can tell all my secrets to without anyone
ever finding them out. God is the therapist who can offer me all the advice and counsel that I need. He is even
the doctor that can heal my body.

When I was in Argentina, I had to seek God on my
own, without mom and dad around to tell me when I
should pray or read my Bible: I had to make a conscious

decision every day to spend time with God because I wanted to, and not because I was told. When I did that, I was finally able to discover God for myself. He was the shoulder I cried on when I felt sad and homesick in Argentina, and my best friend when none of my friends were available to talk to me. The few times I was sick in Argentina, He healed my body. Most importantly, He was and is the I AM, which allows me to trust in Him every day.

God wants to be your everything, too. He is the mender of broken hearts, and as the Alpha and Omega, He knows how you will begin your destiny and how you will finish it. All you have to do is allow Him to be there for you.

Dear Father, I pray this prayer with all sincerity. Come into my life today and be my everything, not just for the major parts of my life, but also for the minor problems that might come my way. I love You God and thank You for being I AM, the Almighty, my God and best friend. I love you and can't wait to see you soon. In Jesus's name, amen.

All Things Are Working for My Good

"And we know that in all things God works for the good of those who love him, who have been called according to his purpose." (Romans 8:28)

When I was in 9th grade, I was on the soccer team. One day, as I was running towards the ball, I was kicked by a girl from the opposing team who was running for the ball as well. Though it was an accident, she kicked me so hard that my knee dislocated. My family rushed me to the hospital; thank God it was only a minor sprain! After two weeks of rest, I was able to play soccer again.

Of course, I did not like beings sidelined for two weeks and I complained about it every day to my friends and family. You know, I think sometimes the devil tries to throw things in our direction to slow us down. It can be an unexpected speeding ticket, a boy or girl that we know is not right for us, an accident, a bad grade in school, or becoming sick. When these unexpected turns come our way, sometimes we complain to God. We think, *Why are you doing this to me?* and automatically blame God instead of trusting His plan for our lives.

Obviously, no one wants to pay that unexpected speeding ticket or retake that class to graduate, but all things are working for good. We may not understand why God allows certain situations to happen to us, but we know that God loves us and wants us to make it into Heaven. So, if a speeding ticket or an illness can bring you closer to Christ, guess what? He is going to allow it to happen. So instead of complaining when unexpected things happen that we may not like, pray and ask God, *What is your will for my life and how will this help bring me closer to you?*

Dear Jesus, help me not to complain and blame You when the devil throws things my way. Help me to cling to You and trust, even though I might be uncomfortable for a while. And Lord, allow me to grow closer to You each day. I love You, and forgive me for my sins. In Jesus name, amen.

Raw Convo with God

What does 'purpose' mean to you, and how do you envision it aligning with God's plan for your life?

A Letter from God to You

"I love those who love me, and those who seek me find me." (Proverbs 8:17)

My daughter, I love you. I have loved you before the earth was formed, before your parents could walk, while you were in your mother's womb--and I love you even now. I love you because you are made in my image. You are a product of me, and I love you because I am love. I know this world is full of sorrow and pain. I know at times you might not feel that I am with you. I know that you are tired and want to give up, but I tell you my child I am with you.

I am with you when you go for that job interview, I am with you when you apply for that college. I am with you in your relationship. I am and will always be with you in any situation bad or good because I love you. There is no other person on this planet that loves you as much as I do. I am the one that sent my only Son down to this sinful earth to die for your sins. All you have to do is believe in me so that when I return you can see me for the first time and have eternal life. My child, I want that for you so much. I just need you to believe in me and know that I will never leave you or forsake you. I love you, and I will always love you because you are my daughter. So don't give up, keep the good fight, and I promise that I will return for you. All you have to do is believe in me as I believe in you, and when the time is right, I will see you soon. I love you my child and I can't wait to hear from you soon.

Sincerely,
Your Father in Heaven, God

Family Time

"A friend loves at all times and a brother is born for a time of adversity." (Proverbs 17:17)

What I love most about the holidays is the family I get to see. Every Thanksgiving and Christmas, my family and I go to my great aunt's house, where we are welcomed by a table of food and a mountain of gifts. My family is the first one to arrive and the last one to leave. From cousins to great aunts--during the holidays, my whole family is there.

Family is very important in a person's life. They are there to cheer you up, pick you up, support you and even fight for you. You may not like your family, or they might get on your nerves, but they are your family forever. Sometimes we take for granted the people who are the dearest in our life because we figure there will always be a tomorrow. Unfortunately, tomorrow is promised to no one. The Bible says, "a brother is born for adversity" (Proverbs 17:17) meaning that your family is there for you when others are not. Life is too short to continue living in this sinful world and allowing days to go by without checking in on family or forgiving our loved ones and moving on.

I challenge you today, even if it is not the holiday season, to reach out to that loved one who might have done you wrong, or to the loved one that you grew apart from. Let them know how you feel and that you want to put aside differences and come together as a family. As the saying goes, "Blood is thicker than water."

Dear Jesus, thank you for giving me a family even if I take them for granted or they get on my nerves. Help me to appreciate them even when I do not want to. Thank You, Lord, for all Your blessings, especially my family. Forgive me for mistreating them and help me to continue to love them as you love me. In Jesus' name, amen.

Get Back Up

"The Lord makes firm the steps of the one who delights in him; though he may stumble, he will not fall, for the Lord upholds him with his hand."

Psalm 37:23-24

Last night while I was cleaning my room, I started singing "We Fall Down" by Donnie McClurkin. As I began to sing the chorus, I stopped at the lyric "For a saint is just a sinner who fell down and got up." Full disclosure--this wasn't my first time hearing this song. My parents played it in the house all the time, I played it at my job on the radio, and I even have the song on my iPhone. But in all the times I have heard or played this song, I never understood that verse until last night.

I immediately stopped what I was doing, ran into my parents' room and told my mother about my realization. In our Christian walk there will be times where we might stumble or fall. It could be anything from being impatient to having premarital sex. God knows us better than we know ourselves. He knows the Christian walk is not a wide, easy road but a narrow and difficult one. There will be obstacles and tests that you will have to face in order to strengthen your walk with God.

The great thing is that God said in His word that He will hold us by the hand during the process. Don't you just love that about God? He will help us through the test and will make sure we pass each test with His guidance. So, the next time you are faced with something, and you stumble a few times, do not give up! Hold on to God's unchanging hand, for we are all sinners, but a Christian is one who fell down and got back up.

Dear Jesus, I know that the Christian path is long and hard road, but I also know if I put my trust in you, I will have the victory over every obstacle that comes my way. I pray that you will continue to guide my footsteps when I stumble and fall. Please be there to pick me up. Forgive me for my sins, in Jesus' name, amen.

A Letter from God

"The Lord our God is merciful and forgiving, even though we have rebelled against him" (Daniel 9:9)

My child I forgive you. I want you to know that no matter what you do, you can always tell me about it and ask for forgiveness. I am not a tyrant that you should be afraid of, I am a father who simply wants the best for his children. My child, I forgive you for the sins you have committed in your past. I forgive you for the ones you did today and the ones you will do tomorrow. I forgive you--and I want you to forgive yourself. I know that you have been through so much in your lifetime. You might have done some things, said some things or even wronged some people, and you may not have the courage to tell me. Well, I am telling you my child, you can come to me. Do not be afraid for I have not given you the spirit of fear. I have given you the spirit of life, light, and love. I am only a prayer away and trust me, I hear everything you say. I know you're ashamed of what you have done. I know that no one knows the deepest darkest, secrets that you wish you didn't carry. I know all these things about you, and I am telling you that I do not look at you any differently.

I see you as a child who needs her father's guidance and reassurance that everything will be okay. And it will be okay, for my word says in Matthew 11:28, "Come unto me, all ye that labor and are heavy laden and I will give you rest." My child that is all I want for you: peace and rest. So tonight, before you go to sleep, talk to me and tell me the things you have done, for I will forgive you Are you ready to be forgiven? I love you my child with all my heart. I forgive you.

Sincerely,
Your Father in Heaven, God

Specific Prayers

"Therefore, I tell you, whatever you ask for in
prayer, believe that you have received it, and it
will be yours" (Mark 11:24)

Often, we underestimate the power of prayer and tend not to pray for the specific things we want in life. For example, we might ask God for a car, but not tell him the brand, year, features of the car, or the mileage. Or we might ask God to help us pass a class, but not specify if we want an A, B, or a C in the class.

I remember my freshman year of college I was in my room thinking about the $3,000 left I had on my tuition in order to clear for the spring semester. I asked God specifically for $3,000 so that I could continue my schooling. Literally two hours later I received a letter saying that I was cleared for the spring semester, and I had a credit of $3.14. It was in that moment that I realized that you have to be specific with your prayers and there is nothing wrong with that.

I have learned over the years that God just wants to see us happy, and He will grant us anything we want as long as it is in His will. We sometimes feel as though God doesn't want to hear the details of our prayers, but he does. He wants to grant you the desires of your heart, but you have to be willing to boldly ask God for what you want. So, the next time you want something, be specific with him and see how He will bless you with the desires of your heart.

Father, I realize that I have been lacking in the prayer department. I realize that it is okay to include the details of what I am praying for in my prayers. Lord, help me to feel comfortable to ask these things from you. In Jesus' name, amen.

His Protection Covers Us

"Be strong and courageous. Do not be afraid or ter-rified because of them for the Lord your God goes with you; he will never leave you nor forsake you."
(Deuteronomy 31:6)

While I was traveling throughout South America, I travelled to Peru and discovered it has some of the best souvenirs. In Peru, I saw a lot of Peruvian arti-facts from boots to jewelry, noticing that the culture is greatly embedded within these objects. As I was doing my shopping, I came across a beautiful turquoise and gold blanket. It was so beautiful, handmade, and most importantly, long enough to cover my entire body and keep it warm from the cold.

It got me thinking. God is like our blanket when we are cold. He covers us and protects us from the wiles of the enemy. God is love, joy, comfort, peace, strength, trust and so much more. All of these different attributes allow God to be our blanket. His word says that He will keep you safe from all hidden dangers and from all deadly diseases. (Psalm 9:13) I do not know about you, but that is a blanket that priceless, and it is all yours.

All you have to do is ask God for His hand of protection to cover you, and He will do that and then some. So, remember if you feel alone, scared, tired or afraid, ask for God to cover you in his unconditional loving and protecting blanket.

Lord come into my life today and cover me with Your protecting hand. I know that the devil is busy and will do anything he can to wipe me out, but I ask You to cover me as a blanket does and keep me safe. Thank You, Jesus, for Your protection and love, in Jesus' name, amen.

A Letter from God

    Why do you continue to hurt me? My child, I love you, and I say this not with judgement, but with concern. Why do you insist on being like the world? You are a child of the King. I am the I AM, yet you continue to look, act, speak, eat, and drink like the world. I came into this world to save you, but I did not conform to this world. I did not go out and party with thieves or smoke with kings or drink with prostitutes. I brought those people to the kingdom by my holy actions. My child, I want what is best for you. I know what is best for you, and the world's clothing does not fit you. I can offer you a fresh white robe with a gold crown full of diamonds, pearls, and gems that you have never dreamed of. I have eternal life, happiness, peace, and love waiting for you. I can and will give you these treasures and much more. The world can only offer you temporary satisfaction, but I can offer eternal everything. Again, I ask why do you insist on being like the world and following its ways? Is it because you want to stay cool? Do you want to fit in? What is it my child? Tell me and together we can fix it. All I want is to be with you and see you, but listen to me. I need you to stop hurting me, especially when you know to do better but you continue to do the same thing. My child, I love you, and I want you to know that I am just a prayer away.

Sincerely,
Your Father, God

Trust the Process. If God Brings You into It, He Will See You Through It

"When you pass through the waters, I will be with you;
and when you pass through the rivers, they will not
sweep over you. When you walk through the fire, you
will not be burned; the flames will not set you ablaze."
Isaiah 43:2

One of the hardest things I have ever done in my 22 years of living is studying abroad. Yes, the traveling, eating, and meeting new people was joyous, but the studying of Spanish was painful. When I arrived in Argentina, I only knew a couple of words. I did not know how to say, "Can you turn off the light?" or "Can I go to the bathroom?" without feeling stupid and nervous all the time. There were times when I wanted to give up because I could not see the progress I was making. At times, I felt as though God did not care how I was feeling because every time I took a step forward it seemed as though I was taking five steps back.

To make things worse, I felt guilty for complaining to God about my situation because a few months before

I was begging God to help me find the funds to travel abroad. I had all these feelings inside of me until one day I was talking to my mom, and she told me "If God brings you to it, He will see you through it". From that moment my prayers changed from "God why?" to "God help me."

In our lives, we are going to go through uncomfortable situations that might have us question, "God why?" It is in these moments that you need to get on your knees and ask God to give you the strength to make it through whatever storm He is bringing you through. Of course, our flesh wants to give up and complain, but God wants us to rely on Him. If I had given up when I was in Argentina, I would not be a 22-year-old bilingual African American woman. Even though the process was hard, I am glad I stayed committed and relied on God because the reward was worth receiving. So remember, whatever you might be going through, hold on, stay strong, trust the process and know that if God brought you to it, He will see you through it. You are not going to fail.

Dear Jesus, help me to rely on you when you bring certain uncomfortable situations into my life. I know now that you will not leave me to fail, and you have my best interest at heart. Lord, help me to trust the process even when I want to give up and complain. In Jesus name, amen.

Raw Convo with God

Reflect on a moment when you felt closest to God. What was happening, and what made that moment so impactful?

Who is in Your Circle?

"Do not be misled: Bad company corrupts good character." (1 Corinthians 15:33)

You know that saying "One bad apple spoiled the bunch"? Well, it is the same with me in my circle of friends. Growing up as a Seventh-day Adventist and going to public school, making friends of good morals and standards was hard at times. I remember in my freshman year of high school there was a group of girls that I started to hang out with. We all know how high school was, a place where everyone wanted to fit in, and unfortunately, I started to fall into that trap.

At the time, I thought the girls I was hanging out with were cool. We would go to class together, eat lunch together, and talk about boys together. As freshman year continued to progress, I started to notice that these girls were into partying, smoking, drinking, and everything else you can imagine. After a while, they had me questioning my morals and values. I knew that I wanted to avoid being labeled as the partying girl or associated with any negative behaviors, as those actions were completely foreign to me and discouraged within my family. My solution was to immediately distance myself from these girls, so I began to hang out with people who were active in extracurricular activities.

Sometimes we underestimate the influences that we can become susceptible to just from the people who we let into our inner circle. We have to realize that not everyone we vibe with, can laugh and crack jokes with is meant to be in our circle of friends. Sometimes people are meant to be acquaintances and just that. The enemy is always looking for a way to snatch us and trap us in his world, but for God's grace He is able to save us from the devil's ways. So if you feel like the friends you are hanging around are not what you want, or you feel like you can't get away from the friendship that is already forming, then ask God to help you and give you the wisdom to distance yourself from these people. Ask Him to bring people in your life that will help build you up and are worth hanging around. Trust me, you are not alone, and if God can do it for me, I know He can do it for you.

Dear Father, I want friends that are going to build me up and bring me closer to you. I do not want negative influences in my inner circle. Give me discernment when it comes to choosing friends and give me the wisdom to distance myself from those I do not want in my inner circle. Thank you, Jesus. In your precious name, Amen.

Judgmental Much?

"When they kept on questioning him, he straight-ened up and said to them, 'If any one of you is with-out sin, let him be the first to throw a stone at her.'"
(John 8:7)

When you look at the bible, Mary Magdalene was one extraordinary woman who overcame a lot of sins and temptation through Jesus, but let's take a look at her life. First, she was possessed with seven demons, and it wasn't until she started to follow Christ that she was released from her bondage. She was the woman who washed and oiled Jesus' feet with her hair. She was also a caught in adultery and charged to be stoned. In today's society, Mary Magdalene could potentially be subjected to derogatory labels or judgements. Imagine Mary coming to church or sitting next to you in your classes! I can only imagine the snickering, comments, and stares she would get, and you would likely partici-pate in the judgments.

My question is, why? Why do we judge those who are struggling in their lives? Why do we as Christians frown upon the teen mom, the recovering drug addict, the locked-up child? Why are we so quick to judge? Is it because their sin is obvious, but ours is secret? No one knows that at night you look at pornography, or that you cheat on your test, or that you're disrespectful to your parents. No one sees the hidden sins that you commit, but as soon as someone makes a mistake that is "very obvious" we like to judge and point the finger.

Those people who were ready to stone Mary did not think twice about their sins because no one knew of them except Jesus. That is why he said, "If any one of you is without sin, let him be the first to throw a stone at her." (John 8:7) It is the same with us. Though we have hidden sins that only God knows of, that does not give us the right to judge someone else's obvious sin. If anything, we should embrace them with love and a godly sprit because if the tables were turned, we would want that to happen to us. We would not want all the stares and snickering but hugs and words of encouragement.

I know I have judged people based on their mistakes, and God said to me, "Who are you to judge? If I was to lay your sins out for the world to see, you would be so embarrassed." It is the same for all of us. So, the next time you feel that comment about to form, or the look turning into a stare, think twice about your life and the sins you are struggling with because, truth be told, no one has room to judge but God himself.

Dear Father, help me not to judge. I know that it can be easy to judge someone else's sins before looking at ourselves first. Help me, Lord, to remember that You are the only one who can judge and give me a more caring and loving heart. In Jesus' name, amen.

Let It Go!

"And when you stand praying, if you hold anything against anyone, forgive them, so that your Father in heaven may forgive you your sins." (Mark 11:25)

One thing that God has been showing me throughout my life is how to forgive and let go. I am the type of person that will remember everything you did wrong towards me and will let it fester inside. God brought this to my attention while I was in college. One day I was relaxing, and I started to think about all the mean things people would say about me, from the color of my skin to my weight. I started to get upset and think about ways I could get back at the people who said these things, whether it was deleting them from Facebook or not liking their pictures on Instagram.

The thing about these memories is that they were from when I was in middle and high school. I was feeling some type of way because I was still harboring ill feelings toward my fellow classmates. It was in that moment that God asked me, "Why are you allowing your mind to think about these things and create vengeful thoughts? You are in college and these people have gone on with their lives. They probably won't even remember you or at least what they used to say about you. It's time to *let it go!*"

You might be reading this and thinking "Really, Faithful ... middle and high school? Y'all were kids, and that is stupid." You're right! It was stupid that I would let something so childish get me upset, but believe it or not, there are a lot of people in this world who harbor little things inside of them for years. When people do us wrong, we tend to keep it bottled up inside instead of forgiving that person and moving on with our lives. You may be tempted to compare trials, and maybe yours is worse: my husband cheated on me, my best friend slept with my boyfriend, my cousin cursed me out, my sister stole all my money. You can even say my rapist raped me as a child, and he was a part of my family. You're right. All of these scenarios and many more are far worse than some middle schoolers picking on each other; however, the principal still remains. Let it go.

God wants us to forgive those who do wrong to us even when we don't want to. By forgiving, we allow ourselves to move on in life and become free from the bondage that is holding us back. Now of course forgiveness takes time, but do not keep that pain, hurt and anger inside forever. Give all those feelings to God, for He wants us to cast our cares upon him. That is what He is there for. I know it might be difficult; it took me almost 10 years to forgive those kids who treated me badly in middle school. If you are having a problem with forgiveness, tell God and he will teach you how to forgive. Trust me, I am still learning myself every day, but the key is to allow God to guide you every step of the way, and I promise you, you will feel so much better once you do.

Dear Jesus, I have a problem with forgiving others who did me wrong. I have tried to move past it, but for some reason I can't seem to. I know that You are a God of forgiveness, so I ask that You take control of my situation. Guide me and teach me how to just let things go whether they are big or small. Thank you, Lord in Jesus' name, amen.

Are You Still Here Listening to Me?

> I cried to him with my mouth, his praise was on my tongue. If I had cherished sin in my heart, the Lord would not have listened. But God has surely listened and has heard my prayer. Praise be to God, who has not rejected my prayer or withheld his love from me!
>
> Psalm 66: 17-20

I have always been a praying woman. Ever since I was a child, I have always tried to strengthen my relationship with God through prayer. One day in particular, I was praying to God about a lot of stuff in my life. I had been asking Him day in and day out for guidance for my schooling, job, friends, family and especially my spiritual life. This prayer was so essential to me because not only was I praying for an hour, but I was looking for answers as to what my next move was going to be. I remember I started to cry to God because I kept asking Him for guidance, and I felt like He wasn't there. I could hear the devil saying, "Look at you praying to a wall and a ceiling. God is not listening to you; He has better things to do."

As soon as I heard that I continued to pray to God even harder and more diligently, asking Him to please grant my prayers and show me the way. It was in that moment I heard God say, "I hear you, Faithful. Just be patient." I felt so much relief after that moment.

God wants me to tell you that He hears you. You might be praying for something to happen, praying for deliverance, praying for a blessing, a miracle, or just a closer walk with God. You might feel as though God isn't listening and that your prayers are hitting the celling and falling down. I assure you: God is listening to your prayers, desires, cries, pain, screaming, laughing, begging, all of it. He hears every plea even before you form the words, and He wants you to trust in Him and rebuke the discouragements that the devil will try to say to you. God has you and He is listening. Remember, He is only one prayer away!

Dear Jesus, thank you for always being a listening ear, even when I feel like you're not listening. I see now that you have my best interest at heart, and you will grant me the desires I have been praying for as long as I stay patient and trust in you. Forgive me for doubting you and continue to help me to trust in you. This I ask in Jesus' name, amen.

Everyone is Watching You. There is Someone Always Watching.

But Ruth replied, "Don't urge me to leave you or to turn back from you. Where you go I will go, and where you stay I will stay. Your people will be my people and your God my God. Where you die I will die, and there I will be buried. May the Lord deal with me, be it ever so severely, if even death separates you and me." When Naomi realized that Ruth was determined to go with her, she stopped urging her.

Ruth 1:16-18

There were many faithful women in the Bible: Esther, Mary, Rebecca, Sarah. But the one I want to talk about today is Ruth. Ruth was a Moabite woman who left everything she knew to follow her mother-in-law, Naomi, to her homeland. Now imagine that your husband has just died, and your whole entire world has been turned upside down. Your mother-in-law says that she is leaving for good, and your sister goes off and does her own thing.

What do you do? Do you go back to your old ways knowing better? Do you follow your mother-in-law?

Or do you marry someone new because you're lonely? Ruth chose to follow her mother-in-law and trusted in the God that was Naomi's God. Ruth did not start with having a strong relationship with God. She didn't know what it meant to pray, trust, and believe. She wasn't taught those values in school. However, because she saw Naomi's actions and the faithfulness she showed to God even in her sorrow, Ruth was able to trust in a God she did not know completely.

Over time, she strengthened her relationship with God. If it wasn't for Naomi being a faithful servant to God and obeying his commands, Ruth probably wouldn't have followed Naomi back to Bethlehem. It is the same in our lives. We have friends and family members who are watching us to see how we will serve God. They are waiting to see if we are going to forget about God and do our own thing or cling to His word, especially when disaster hits us. Our actions affect the people we love every day. The question is are you going to be an example for God's children or are you going to be like the world?

Dear Jesus, I know a lot of people are watching me, and sometimes it is annoying. I want to bring others to You, so I am asking that you will guide me so that my actions are revealing of you. Thank you, Jesus, in your precious name, amen.

Raw Convo with God

Describe a time when you felt unsure about your purpose or direction in life. How did you seek clarity or guidance from God during that period?

Being Faithful and Consistent

"I thank Christ Jesus our Lord, who has given me strength, that he considered me trustworthy, appointing me to his service" (I Timothy 1:12)

A few summers ago, I decided to do a workout challenge. The workout included 5-6 videos of different dances that I had to complete in order to lose weight. Now I love to exercise, especially cardio. As the summer went by, I continued to do the different exercise videos, and by the time summer ended, I lost the weight.

The key to exercising is staying consistent to the workout plan. There were days I wanted to give up or eat some food that I knew was unhealthy for my body. There were even days I wanted to quit, but I didn't. I stayed faithful to the workout plan even when I felt like I wasn't seeing results.

It is the same way in our walk with God. We sometimes feel as though we are not seeing the fruits of our labor. We have our devotionals, pray every day, and go to church every Sabbath but still wonder where are the blessings God said he would provide? When can I get the victory over this relationship, class, job, or even family member?

God wants you to know that if you are faithful in the littlest of things, he will make you faithful in many. Don't become weary in doing good. Continue being consistent in your prayers, devotions, tithing and offerings, as well as your relationship with God. Trust me, God will show up when you least expect it. The key is consistency.

Dear Jesus, help me to stay consistent to you even when I get discouraged. Continue to help me in my walk with You, in Jesus' name, amen.

Cleaning Day

"Wash away all my iniquity and cleanse me from my sin." (Psalms51:2)

The other day, I woke up early in the morning, with a sore throat and clogged nose. I did not know how this happened because before I went to bed, I felt fine. I searched my parents' room for Vicks and when I found it, I put it on my chest, throat, and nose. When that did not help, I rubbed some essential oils on my forehead and temples, but they did not relieve the pressure either.

At this point, my nose was so clogged that I couldn't smell the Vicks or the essential oils. I began to search the apartment for anything that could relieve my misery. I went to the linen closet and in the top shelf I found a sinus rinse with over 50 packs of solution. A sinus rinse is a rinse for the nose. It has a bottle with saline solution that you mix with warm water. I immediately began to assemble the bottle. Then, I proceeded to rinse my nose. As I was going through the rinsing process, it was very uncomfortable. There was a lot of water coming out of my nose and mouth, and I felt that the solution was not working because I could still feel my stuffed-up nose.

After finishing the rinse, I washed the bottle out and went on with my day. When I got down the hall, I noticed that my sore throat and stuffy nose was gone! It is the same way in our Christian walk with God. We sometimes do not notice the cleansing process God is leading us through. We feel as though nothing is happening because we do not see fast results. We tend to give up on God or get mad because we want to get through the storm now. God wants you to know that if you remain faithful to Him, you will soon see results in your spiritual journey. So don't be discouraged, hold on, and allow God to clean the mess out of your life today.

Dear Jesus, I realize that You have to clean me and get rid of some things that are not like You. Lord, I ask that You will continue to give me patience during this time. You know I like fast results, but help me to trust in You during this process and know that Your timing is the best timing. Forgive me if I ever try to speed up the process. In Jesus' name, amen.

Timing is Everything

"Why, you do not even know what will happen to-morrow. What is your life? You are a mist that appears for a little while and then vanishes." (James 4:14)

One thing that waits for no man is time. My mom used to say if the game starts at 10, you don't arrive at 10, you arrive at 9. I used to procrastinate to the 11th hour of everything. I could have papers and projects due and while everyone else was getting a head start, I was chilling in my bed watching TV. My procrastination did not truly start affecting me till I was in my junior and senior year of high school. Those two years were very important because I was starting to look at colleges.

I remember I had a seven-page AP Literature paper due. Now this paper wasn't your average paper. I had to do a lot of research, go in depth about my position on the topic and have facts to back it up: a lot of work. I literally waited until the night before it was due to start the project, and I did not go to bed until 4 that morning. On top of that, I had to present my paper to the class, and I had forgotten all about that until my teacher called my name. Thank God, I have a wonderful memory and

I was able to finesse my way through the presentation, but my research paper did not receive as much grace as my verbal presentation. Suffice to say, the grade I received was far below acceptable standards, and from that day forward, I told myself I would not procrastinate again. God wants us to use our time wisely. We have 24 hours in a day, and most of those hours are not used successfully. God values time and wants us to use it wisely. So the next time you have to do something, get it done right then and there; do not wait till the last minute.

Lord, help me to use my time wisely for You and other aspects in my life. I know I can be lazy and let the hours pass me by, but I am seeking for Your guidance to manage my time wisely. Thank you, Lord for your help, in Jesus' name, amen.

Raw Convo with God

How do you navigate challenges while seeking God's guidance and strength in your college journey

Self-Control

"But the fruit of the Spirit is love, joy, peace, for-bearance, kindness, goodness, faithfulness, gentle-ness, and self-control. Against such things there is no law." (Galatians 5: 22-23)

Brazil was one of the countries where I truly savored the food. I remember going to a pizza buffet with some of my friends, and that night was the night of my life. I love to eat at buffets, and my favorite food is pizza, so being able to enjoy both food options for the price of one was a real treat. Once we were seated, the waiters came out with all different types of pizza, from spinach and cheddar to regular cheese pizza. They even threw in chicken and steak pieces as well.

By the fifth round I was starting to get full, but for some reason I did not want to stop. I was determined to try every pizza that they had to offer. Around the 10th round the desserts started to come out. Pizza desserts! Mind you my stomach was full at this point, but I did not stop. I simply unbuckled my pants and proceeded with dinner. The rounds went up to 20, and I made it to round 18. By the end of the night, I had a terrible headache. I was constipated, and I had a stomachache. I just wanted to go home and sleep.

The reason I continued to eat after I was full is because I did not have self-control. When you think about self-control, most people think about controlling your anger or temper, and that is true, but how often do we practice self-control in our appetites? Having a gluttonous spirit is a sin and God doesn't want us to lose self-control when we are faced with food. If I would have used self-control while eating, I could have saved myself a headache and a stomachache. The next time you are faced with a situation, and you want to lose self-control, remember the fruits of the spirit. God wants you to have control over yourself so that when you are faced with temptation you will be able to control yourself.

Lord, I see that I need to have self-control in my life. I know that you are preparing me for the future, and I have to learn how to control my anger, hunger, emotions, and everything for Your glory. Help me, Lord, to practice self-control even when I don't want to. Thank you, Lord. In Jesus' name, amen.

Grace and Mercy

Three times I pleaded with the Lord to take it away from me. But he said to me, "My grace is sufficient for you, for my power is made perfect in weakness. "Therefore, I will boast all the more gladly about my weaknesses, so that Christ's power may rest on me. That is why, for Christ's sake, I delight in weaknesses, in insults, in hardships, in persecutions, in difficulties. For when I am weak, then I am strong.

2 Corinthians 12:8-10

One of the most traumatic events I have experienced was a car accident with my two little sisters. On December 2, 2016, I was driving around the neighborhood with my sisters to get something to eat. We were talking about life, and just enjoying each other's company at a stop light when all of a sudden, we heard BOOM! I blacked out for a couple of seconds, and once I regained consciousness, I immediately got my sisters and myself out the car and proceeded to call our parents. The paramedics arrived immediately and started to ask questions about the vehicle. I did not even realize we were in an accident until a lady told me.

Turns out we were rear ended at stop light by a woman who was on meth. Once the police told me that information, I immediately started crying and thanking Jesus for saving our lives. Yes, we had a couple of broken bones, bumps, and bruises, but I was so thankful that it wasn't more serious. God and His angels saved our lives that night. The back of the van that I was driving was completely totaled. It was totaled to the point that if it wasn't for God's protection, we would have died.

Every day the devil tries to take our lives. Sometimes it might be obvious like a car accident, or a sickness. And other times it's not so obvious. God is always protecting us even when we don't deserve it. He protects us because He loves us, He protects us because He wants us to get our lives right with Him, and He protects us because He is our Father, and a father always protects his children. You might have experienced a traumatic near-death experience like I did, and God saw fit to save your life, or maybe you've never been through an experience like mine, but you know you need to make some changes to your life. Whichever one it is, make sure you are right with God. That accident was a wakeup call for my life as well as my sisters'.

I never thought that I would experience a terrible accident, especially with my two younger sisters. I thank God every day that I'm alive, and I have another day to get it right with God. If you feel like you need to get it right with God, do it now! Because tomorrow is not promised to anyone, and in a split second your life can change forever.

Dear Jesus, thank you for protecting me every day even though I don't deserve it. I know that I haven't been completely 100 percent with You, but I am willing to change. I want to be saved in Your kingdom so that in person I can say thank You. But for now, I'm saying thank You for all You've done and all You continue to do. In Jesus' name, amen.

Love Yourself

"I praise you because I'm fearfully and wonderfully made; your works are wonderful; I know that full well." (Psalms 139:14)

I had a friend who always saw something wrong with herself. Every time we would go somewhere, whether it was shopping or to an event, she always would complain about how ugly she looked, or how fat she was. At first, I tried to ignore it or compliment her to boost her self-esteem, but soon my patience was starting to run out. The negative energy that I was getting from her was annoying and starting to make me question myself as to how I looked. One day I pulled her aside and had a talk with her on how her words weren't only affecting the way she saw herself, but also the way I saw her. I told her, "If you do not find yourself beautiful, then no one will." Acceptance of yourself starts with you.

Ladies, we all have insecurities about our bodies. We are human, and it is normal. When you allow your insecurities to affect the way you view yourself 24/7, you begin to believe that you are ugly, you are fat, or you are too skinny. Unfortunately, we allow the media to tell us what is considered pretty and ugly; it begins to affect how we see ourselves. God made you beautiful just the way you are.

Now of course we all have heard that saying, but it is true. God knows that your hair texture fits you perfectly. He knew your shoe size would make your feet look pretty. He knew the color of your skin would make you unique. Remember there is no other girl, like you on this planet. God made you special in your own way, and if God, the creator whose opinion should truly matter in your life, says you are beautiful, then believe it.

Dear Jesus, I haven't accepted myself for who I am. I have fought with the body You have given me. I know the media can portray what's beautiful, and unfortunately, I have believed them. Lord, thank you for making me the woman I am today and help me, Lord, to accept who I am and love myself because if You love me for who I am, then I should love myself. Continue to show me why You made me this way, and thank You Lord for making me. In Jesus' name, amen.

Raw Convo with God

Reflect on a Bible verse or story that has significantly impacted your faith journey. Why is it meaningful to you?

A Letter from God

My beautiful daughter, I have so many plans for your life. I want to take you to places humanity has never dreamed of. I want you to accomplish goals that your friends, family, and haters said you couldn't do. I want you to prosper. I want you to shine so that others will see my glory and my love in you. I know right now you can't see the plans I have. You might be thinking,

Why is God putting me through this trial? I know it can be discouraging and even scary, but if only you knew how close you were to the finish line. Life is a race where there are hurdles, twists and turns, but my Word is true. James 1:12 says, "Blessed is the man who remains steadfast under trial, for when he has stood the test he will receive the crown of life, which God has promised to those who love him." This is what I have waiting for you, but much more. All you have to do is trust the process, trust me, and obey my voice. Even when in doubt, seek me.

When you want to give up, lean on me. When you want to vent, tell me. I know the plans I have for you, and trust me, my daughter, if you stay faithful to me, I will exalt you. So, remember, my child, I have not forgotten you, for I am with you always, even when you feel like I'm not. You are mine, and because you are mine, I will take care of you. All you have to do is trust what I am doing and listen to me.

Sincerely,
Your Father, God

A Virtuous Woman

"Charm is deceptive, and beauty is fleeting; but a woman who fears the Lord is to be praised." (Proverbs 31:30)

What is the true definition of a virtuous woman? One might say she is a woman who prays all the time. Another might say she is a woman who goes to church and sings in the choir every Saturday. You might even say, "Not me because of the sins I have committed." The truth is a virtuous woman is a woman who fears the Lord and obeys his word. A woman who loves God and serves him with all her heart, soul, and mind. A woman who is a sinner but is saved by grace. She is a woman like you and me.

Many times, we allow our past sins and temptations to distract us. We compare ourselves to other women in the church who might be in the choir, on the pulpit, teaching Sabbath school, etc. We forget that we are all sinners, and because of that, we are all equal. Being a virtuous woman does not mean you are perfect; it means to live life with purpose, diligence, forgiveness, and repentance. So what are some ways we as women can make sure we are being virtuous in our day-to-day life?

1. Keep God at the center of your life. The older we get, the wickeder the world becomes, it is imperative that we include God in every decision that we make for our lives. We have to make sure He is the one guiding us and not the devil.
2. Stay healthy. Our bodies are not ours, but God's. As a result, we must care for them by feeding them the proper nutrients, exercising daily, and getting the proper rest.
3. Serve God. We must remember that our duty as Christians is to serve God, and by serving God, we serve others in the community.

The list goes on and on. There are many ways we can be virtuous women. If you feel like this message applies to you, talk to God about it. If you feel like you need to be a better virtuous woman, start making changes in your life and ask God for help.

Dear Father, help me to continue to live a virtuous life. I know that it can be hard at times, but I am willing to make the change because You are there for me and love me. I love you, always. In Jesus name, amen.

God is An Artist

"Lord, you are my God; I will exalt you and praise your name, for in perfect faithfulness you have done wonderful things, things planned long ago."
(Isaiah 25:1)

Have you looked at a sunset and been so amazed by its orange, purple, blue, yellow, and red colors? Have you ever thought how God allows such simple colors to form a beautiful canvas? Often, we don't see God as an artist, but He is. I mean, look at the world! There is so much natural beauty, from gardens to waterfalls. Even in the Bible, when God created the earth, the description and elements that He used to create this world were unexplainable.

When I was in Argentina, I went to a famous waterfall attraction called Las Cataratas. It was a national waterfall park with different waterfalls, and I thought to myself, *God is such an artist.* I loved the fact that God decided to share his artistic ways with us, because imagining a world without a sunset, moonlight, or hilltop view just makes me sad. This world would be very boring to the eye without God's artistry. Just think, God saw fit to place you on this earth so that you could experience his artistry as well.

Dear Jesus, thank you for the natural art You have placed on this earth. I know I have taken it for granted in the past, but I see that You just wanted us to enjoy what You see in heaven all the time. Lord, I will start to appreciate your works more. Thank You for putting me on this earth so I could enjoy them. In Jesus name, amen.

Raw Convo with God

What are your spiritual gifts, and how do you envision using them to serve others and glorify God?

Fear Not

"Have I not commanded you? Be strong and coura-
geous. Do not be and do not be discouraged for the
LORD your God will be with you wherever you go. "
(Joshua 1 :9)

Joshua was the chosen leader for the Israelites after
Moses. He was told by God to lead the Israelites into the
promised land. Can you imagine the pressure Joshua
must have felt? I mean, he was coming after the proph-
et Moses who led the Israelites out of Egypt. Moses,
the man who saw God's back and countless times, was
in the presence of God. I can just imagine the doubt,
anxiety, and fear that Joshua must have felt, but Joshua
did not let the fear of failure scare him away. In fact, he
faced it because he had God's blessing and help that allowed him to overcome any negative feelings he might
have felt.

Because of Joshua's courage, and with God's help, he
was able to lead the children of Israel into the promised
land, a goal that the great Moses could not complete
himself. If Joshua had been scared about taking on the
leadership after Moses, the Israelites could have wan-
dered in the wilderness for a longer period. They could

have been captured and sold into slavery again, or they could have died off. Honestly, we can come up with so many scenarios as to what would have happened if Joshua had allowed fear take over his judgment.

It is the same in our lives, sometimes we allow fear to get the best of us, and we miss out on our blessing. God wants us to be courageous and brave, but if we let the turmoil of life make us fearful, how can God use us? We are God's children, and He is looking for some Joshuas who are going to stand up and fight for him. He is looking for a Joshua who will take leadership even when you feel like you can't. He is looking and waiting for someone to continue preaching His gospel across the world. Are you that person? If so, go before the throne of God and tell Him.

Lord, help me not to be fearful of different obstacles that might come my way. Give me courage and boldness to continue preaching Your gospel to the world. Thank You for being there for me and continue to help me as I declare my love for You.

You Are a Queen

"So you were adorned with gold and silver; your clothes were of fine linen and costly fabric and embroidered cloth. Your food was honey, olive oil and the finest flour. You became very beautiful and rose to be a queen." (Ezekiel 16:13)

Almost every little girl's dream is to be a queen. I remember my sisters and I used to dress up like queens and parade around the house with our blankets over our heads. Growing up, I thought in order to be a queen you had to live in a castle and have servants and maids and, of course, be filthy rich. But I know now that is not necessarily true, even though I am just a 22-year-old woman in college, I am a queen.

You know what makes me a queen? The way I view myself and who my Father is. You see, I have a Father that sits high and looks low. My Father has riches, above anything anyone on earth can have. My Father has worlds that are not of this world, and it is only a matter of time until I get to see them. And the best part is, my Father is also your Father, which makes you royalty and a queen as well.

See, I may not have a castle on this earth, but I know in the earth made new there's already one with my name on it. I may not have the riches of an earthly queen, but in heaven I am going to have far more than riches can buy. I may not even look like royalty on this earth, but my God knows my worth and knows I am royalty material.

You are a queen as well. God is your father as much as He is mine. He has that house or even castle for you. He has the riches and wealth that you seek. He has it all, and guess what. It is all free. God just says come as you are, and the rest is yours. So, the next time you see a magazine with the royal family on it, remember you are royalty as well, and God has all your riches in heaven. All you must do is ask and accept Him as your Lord and Savior.

Thank you, God, for making me royalty and accepting me for who I am. Help me to see myself as a queen even when I don't feel like it. Save me Lord so when You come, I can gain the riches you have for me in heaven. In Jesus name, amen.

Don't Go Back!

"Forget the former things; do not dwell on the past.
See, I am doing a new thing! Now it springs up; do
you not perceive it? I am making a way in the wil-
derness and streams in the wasteland." (Isaiah 43:
18—19)

I do not know what God has delivered you from, but do not go back to whatever it was.

Maybe it was a relationship, or a friend, or a toxic situation. Whatever it might have been, God saw it fit to rescue you. Sometimes we get so used to our toxic situation that when God rescues us, we want to go back. I remember how the Israelites wanted to be free so badly, but once they were free and in the wilderness, they started to complain and wanted to go back to Egypt. Do you know how stupid is it to go back to slavery because you're tired of being free? That's how we are when it comes to God. We want God to rescue us, but once He does, if we are uncomfortable about the situation we start wanting to go back.

For example, you knew that guy was not good for you, and you begged God to help you out of the situation, and He did. Now a month has passed, and you are starting to miss him, and call him on the phone. Another example is those friends you used to hang out with, who were doing everything wrong. You knew their standards were not your standards.

You asked God to help you make new friends and He did, but your new friends aren't the turn-up type. Instead, they're more of the Bible studying AYS type. So, you begin to miss your old friends and their ways. The list goes on and on. Whatever the situation is or whoever the person is, *don't go back!* God has bigger and better plans for you and wants you to realize that He is taking you to another level—a level that those friends, that boy, and those distractions can't reach. So, trust the process and do not go back to what God delivered you from.

Dear Jesus, help me not go back to what you have delivered me from, whether it's friends, family, things, or relationships. Help me to trust in You throughout the process and rely on Your judgment and not my own. In Jesus name, amen.

Raw Convo with God

In what ways do you currently cultivate a personal relationship with Jesus? How can you deepen this connection further?

I Am a Finisher

"I have fought the good fight, I have finished the course, I have kept the faith." (2 Timothy 4:7)

Life is like a race. There are many obstacles along the way, hurdles that we have to jump, and people that are on our team that we must depend on. The thing about races is they can be tiresome. You might feel like quitting or giving up. You might feel like your race isn't important to finish. Do not give up based on how you are feeling!

God has you in the palm of his hand. He sees the hurdles you will have to overcome, the jumps you will have to make, and the people you will have to recruit on your team. The enemy would love to have you give up because he knows that if you complete this race, you will be one step closer to God. I have run so many races in my life and almost thought of quitting. I know how it feels to wake up every morning and feel like giving up. God showed me that His plans are way bigger for me. If I remain faithful to Him by completing this race, He will remain faithful to me. So, remember to complete the race because you are a finisher in every aspect of your life. You know what it is, and God knows as well.

So tonight, when you talk to Him make sure you tell Him, "I am going to finish this race."

Dear Jesus, I pray that You will give me the strength and courage to finish this race You have for me. Life can be hard and challenging at times, but I know You wouldn't give me more than I can bear. Be with me, Lord, and guide my footsteps as I finish this race. In Jesus' name, amen.

Godly Affirmations for Daily Use

1. I am a powerful God-fearing woman.

2. The spirit of discernment is so heavy upon me. No one can interrupt what Jesus and I have in unity.

3. The Holy Spirit lives inside me

4. The Holy Spirit breathes inside me.

5. The Holy Spirit speaks through me.

6. God answers all my prayers.

7. Everything I want and desire, Jesus gives to me.

8. God has given me gifts that I use for his kingdom.

9. God has made me a very powerful and influential woman.

10. God has qualified me to be in positions of leadership, power, and prosperity.

11. I have a healthy eating lifestyle.

12. I am in control of my emotions and spending habits.

13. I do not excessively emotionally eat.

14. I love to budget.

15. I am a great and successful woman of God.

16. I am the definition of success.

17. I am the definition of Top Tier

18. God provides all my needs.

19. I am humbled and willing to serve God in my everyday life.

20. I love serving Jesus.

21. Jesus is my everything.

22. God cares for me.

23. I care about my relationship with Jesus.

24. I trust Jesus.

25. I know Jesus.

26. I love Jesus.

27. I crave Jesus.

28. I need Jesus.

29. I can do all things through Christ, who strengthens me.

30. When strangers meet me, they immediately meet the Jesus inside of me.

31. I am saved because of Jesus.

32. I care about others.

33. I love others.

34. I am loved.

35. My family loves me.

36. I am attracting my husband into my life.

37. I am mentally OK.

38. I am thriving, living, and breathing.

39. I am a queen.

40. I have positive healthy boundaries, relationships, friendships, coworkers, and business partners.

41. I love to communicate my boundaries.

42. I love to communicate my feelings with others.

43. I like to let people get to know me by communicating my boundaries.

44. I am successful at communicating.

45. I am a magnet for success.

46. I am a magnet for beauty, wealth, power, joy, peace, patience and self-control, all rooted in Jesus Christ.

47. I am a magnet for natural God-given beauty.

48. God has made me a beautiful woman.

49. I wear God's beauty on me.

50. I wear God's perfume or me.

51. God's sweet aroma is drenched on me like no other.

52. I attract God-fearing, like-minded people into my life.

53. I love people from all walks of life.

54. I forgive.

55. I move on.

56. I let go what doesn't fit my life anymore.

57. I trust God.

58. My tongue is a tongue of love.

59. My God is bigger and greater than any devil, demon, evil spirit, or principality.

60. God is creating generational wealth with me.

61. My mind is beautiful.

62. Victory is mine.

63. Peace is mine.

64. Joy is mine.

65. Faith is mine.

66. I have so much faith in God it can move heaven and earth.

67. God provides for all of my needs.

68. Whatever I do prospers.

69. I am God's favorite daughter.

70. Everything I want and desire and am praying for, I already have.

71. I am Top-Tier

72. Jesus is my all.

Afterword

Congratulations on completing this 30-day journey of faith! As we draw the curtains on this devotional, I want to extend my heartfelt gratitude for joining me on this transformative adventure. I pray that these past thirty days have been a catalyst for your spiritual growth and a source of renewed inspiration in your relationship with Jesus Christ.

Remember, the conclusion of these daily reflections doesn't mark the end of your walk with Christ but rather a new beginning. As you step forward from this devotional experience, carry with you the lessons learned, the prayers prayed, and the scriptures that resonated with your soul.

Continuously seek moments of reflection and communion with Jesus, for His love and guidance are steadfast and enduring. Let the truths discovered within these pages remain close to your heart as you navigate the intricacies of college life and beyond.

May your faith continue to flourish, your relationship with Jesus deepen, and your journey be guided by His unwavering love and grace.

Thank you again for embarking on this faith-filled journey. May you walk in the assurance that Christ is always by your side.

The Lord bless you and keep you; the Lord make his face shine on you and be gracious to you; the Lord turn his face toward you and give you peace.

Numbers 6:24-26

About the Author

Faithful Byrd, a multifaceted Christian artist, was born in Hammond, Louisiana and spent her formative years in Suitland, Maryland (also known as the DMV) before embarking on a transformative journey that eventually led her to Orlando, Florida. Her migration to Florida amid the challenges of the COVID-19 pandemic marked a pivotal moment in her academic pursuits, as she pursued her second master's degree at AdventHealth University.

Her educational journey reflects a diverse and accomplished background. She earned a bachelor's degree in TV Broadcast and Spanish from Oakwood University and furthered her studies, acquiring her first master's in organizational management from Andrews University. Additionally, she holds a second master's degree in health administration from AdventHealth, University further enriching her expertise in healthcare management.

Faithful's life has been intertwined with music and ministry since an early age. From singing since the tender age of two, to penning her thoughts and songs at the age of four, her musical gifts and writing abilities became integral parts of her life. She serves as a Christian gospel artist within the Orlando community, sharing her testimony through her ministry called "FaithfulByrdMusic." Through her music, writings, and speeches, she testifies about the goodness of God, reflecting her profound faith in Jesus Christ.

Beyond her artistic endeavors, Faithful Byrd has had diverse experiences. As a 9th-grade English teacher, she serves as an influential mentor to the next generation. Additionally, she extends her talents beyond music and ministry into the realm of business as she serves as a business owner and founder of FB Rentals, utilizing her expertise in property management.

Her passion for God's work and the inspiration for this book stems from her study abroad trip to Argentina. In a foreign country where language barriers existed, Faithful's quest to understand and know God on a deeper level became a defining chapter in her spiritual journey. This book encapsulates her college experiences, chronicling her unwavering faith in God and how it continues to fortify her as she navigates life's peaks and valleys.

Above all titles and accomplishments, Faithful Byrd identifies herself as a child of God, drawing strength and inspiration from her unyielding faith. Her life's journey, enriched with musical notes, testimonies, and spiritual revelations, stands as a testament to God's unwavering grace and goodness in her life and the lives of others.

Milton Keynes UK
Ingram Content Group UK Ltd.
UKHW021935130824
446844UK00008B/586